WARBIRDS ILLUSTRATED No 31

Air War over GERMANY

THE USAAF BOMBING CAMPAIGN
1944–1945

JEFFREY L. ETHELL

ARMS AND ARMOUR PRESS
London · Melbourne · Harrisburg, Pa · Cape Town

Introduction

Published in Great Britain by Arms and Armour Press, Lionel Leventhal Limited, 2–6 Hampstead High Street, London NW3 1QQ. 11 Munro Street, Port Melbourne 3207, Australia. Cameron & Kelker Streets, P.O. Box 1831, Harrisburg, Pa., U.S.A. Sanso Centre, 8 Adderley Street, P.O. Box 94, Cape Town 8000, South Africa.

British Library Cataloguing in Publication Data:
Ethell, Jeffrey
Air war over Germany: the USAAF bombing campaign 1944–1945. – (Warbirds illustrated; no. 31)
1. United States, Air Force – History
2. World War, 1939–1945 – Aerial operations,
American 3. World War, 1939–1945 – Europe
4. Bombers
I. Title II. Series
940.54′21 D790
ISBN 0-85368-700-5

Editing, design and artwork by Roger Chesneau.
Printed in Italy
by Tipolitografia G. Canale & C. S.p.A. - Turin
in association with Keats European Ltd.

Although the major turning points of the Second World War had taken place by 1943, the enormous engine of destruction that had been set in motion in 1939 roared on until 1945. The Allies had faced the possibility of sound defeat early in the war, but they pooled their resources and energies until the Axis was powerless before them.

In 1944 the air war over Europe turned into a battle to the death between Germany, and the Allied powers, spearheaded by the United States and Britain; the USAAF alone brought the 8th and 9th Air Forces to bear from England and the 12th and 15th Air Forces from Italy. The Luftwaffe was hammered down continually, but its pilots rose to do battle against a massive aerial armada, which suffered up until the last days of the war. With the introduction of the ultimate in piston-engine aircraft and the new jet-powered machines, and as thousands of aircraft clashed in the skies, Germany became an aerial battleground the like of which will never be witnessed again.

This book is a glimpse of that time, from D-Day to the fall of Berlin, when men died for the countries they served in spite of often overwhelming odds.

Jeffrey Ethell

◀2
1. (Title spread) The 2nd BG, formed up, climbs out of Foggia in the early morning. Holding tight formation for hour after hour was not only exhausting but also nerve-racking when flak began to find the bombers high overhead. (USAF)
2. A weapon born of desperation, the Bachem Natter vertically launched rocket fighter was designed for the point defence of important targets. The pilot was to fire 24 missiles from the nose, then bail out. A small Natter unit became operational near Stuttgart in April 1945 but never saw action. (USAF)

▲3 ▼4

3. Before the beaches were hit on D-Day, photo reconnaissance units provided extensive information on German movements and plans. Here, Lt. Col. James G. Hall, commander of the 7th Photo Group, briefs his pilots at Mount Farm, England. (USAF)
4. The classic 'buzz job' was something few pilots could resist during the war. This 7th PhG F-5E roars in low over the snow at an 8th Air Force bomber base in England, its pilot giving onlookers some idea of his aircraft's performance. (Roger Freeman)
5. A 7th Photo Group F-5 Lightning alone over the Continent.

Recce pilots did not carry guns, relying instead on speed, altitude and skill to evade German fighters. (7th PhG Archives)
6. Lockheed's P-38 Lightning was introduced into the ETO (European Theatre of Operations) as a long-range escort fighter to protect the bombers, but it was ill-suited for extended, high-altitude flying. This P-38J served with the 554th Squadron, 496th Fighter Group, as an 8th AF operational trainer before pilots were transferred to a front-line unit. (Ray Weinkauf via Mike O'Connor)

▲7

▲8　▼9

7,8. In 1943 Germany was testing the future with jet- and rocket-powered aircraft. This is the Messerschmitt Me 262 V3, the first prototype of the series to fly on jet power alone; next year the 262 would be introduced into combat against the Allied bomber streams. (Via Ken Bokleman)

9. The Luftwaffe was already spread too thin on many fronts in 1944, but its pilots were nevertheless pulled back into Germany to defend the homeland. Here, with his Focke Wulf Fw 190A on standby, ground power plug in and ready for start, Heinz Henke, Adjutant of *Jagdgeschwader 1*, waits on a bright summer day for the next air battle. (Alfred Price)

10. A 20th Fighter Group P-38H at King's Cliffe being readied for a mission. The boots at the bottom of the ladder attest to the ground crew's respect for the fighter. (USAF)

11. As more and more aircraft were shipped to England for increased operations, VIII Air Service Command assembled, modified and test-flew the machines before they went to combat units. This Lightning is being serviced at Burtonwood prior to being delivered to a fighter group. (USAF)

12,13,14. With pieces falling off his aircraft, a Messerschmitt Bf 109 pilot bails out after an attack by an 8th Air Force fighter. (USAF)

15. While an Fw 190 closes on a Lancaster, an Allied fighter catches it by surprise. As confidence grew in being able to hit Germany by daylight, the RAF launched numerous daytime raids.

16. To counter the Allied bombing effort, *Sturmstaffel 1* was formed and equipped with heavily armed and armoured Fw 190As. This Focke Wulf of the unit is seen at Leipzig in October 1944. (Oscar Boesch)

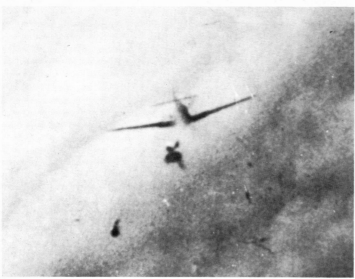

▲12

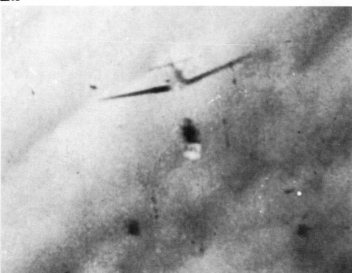

▲13   ▼14

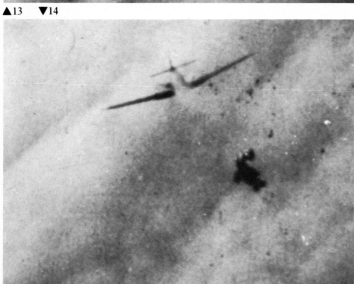

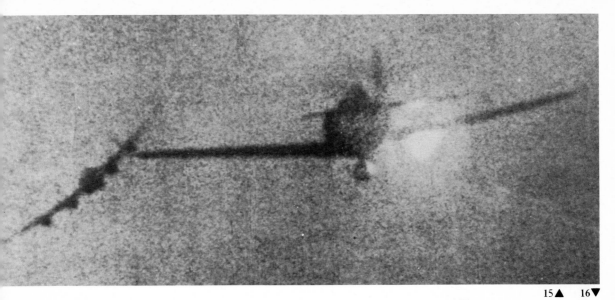

▲17

17. This 95th Bomb Group B-17 was shot down in
May 1944 by a *Sturmstaffel 1* pilot named Schmidt.
The photograph was taken by Schmidt's fellow pilots
as they examined the victory. (Oscar Boesch)

18. The P-51 of 9th AF ace George Preddy being
serviced on a forward strip in France. The black and
white invasion stripes were painted on all Allied
aircraft to help friendly gunners identify enemy
machines – anything without stripes was to be shot at.
(Paul Coggan)

19. After the beachhead was established in June 1944,
the 9th Air Force began to move into quickly
prepared forward air bases to hit tactical targets. This
A-20 was the first to complete 100 missions and was
renamed to commemorate the liberation of France.
(USAF)

▲20

▲21 ▼22

20. The 364th Fighter Group, 8th AF, flew this field-modified F-5E with a non-standard gun arrangement: either the 20mm cannon has been moved further out or a .50 calibre gun has been installed in its place. (Roger Freeman)

21. A 385th Bomb Group B-17G being watched over by a 'little friend' of the 357th Fighter Group low over the English countryside. The sight of a P-51 this close warmed the heart of every bomber crewman. (T. R. Bennett)

22. Oscar Boesch, a pilot with *Sturmstaffel 1*, boards his Fw 190A in 1944. Note the heavy armour glass on the sides of the cockpit. (Oscar Boesch)

23. 'Lucky Wabbit II' flew with the 343rd Squadron, 55th Fighter Group, out of Wormingford. The 'bubble' canopy of the P-51D gave pilots excellent visibility for air combat. (T. R. Bennett)

24. Unlike the other fighter units in the 8th Air Force, the 357th Fighter Group continued to camouflage its new P-51Ds with RAF green and sky. 'Passion Wagon' was flown by ace Arval Roberson out of Leiston. (Arval Roberson)

25. As Allied armies pressed through France and into Germany, the Luftwaffe produced fighter-bombers in ever increasing numbers. This Fw 190G-3 could carry a combination of bombs and external fuel tanks in addition to its fixed armament. When flown by pilots with some experience, it was an effective ground attack aircraft. (George Petersen)

23▲

24▲ 25▼

▲ 26

▲ 27   ▼ 28

26. The skies over Germany became unsafe for anything, even training aircraft. Here a student pilot in an Arado Ar 96 advanced trainer is in bad trouble under the guns of a P-47. The AAF caption noted the aircraft as an Me 109 but one can be sure the German knew better as he tried to get away. (USAF)

27. Maj. Bert Marshall of the 355th Fighter Group brings his crippled Mustang down for belly landing at Steeple Morden after a particularly harrowing mission. (Bill Marshall)

28. The words written by Cpl. Joseph Correa on the interrogation board at this 8th AF bomber base could not be more welcome, particularly since the mission was flown to Berlin. (USAF)

29. The operations room of the 65th Fighter Wing, Saffron Walden, Essex, in 1944. Just as the RAF directed its fighters during the Battle of Britain, the 8th Air Force kept track of its roving pilots as they left to do battle. (USAF)

30. The 65th Fighter Wing's plotting table and route map keeps track of the 4th, 56th, 355th, 361st and 479th Fighter Groups as they head out to escort B-17s and B-24s over Germany. A total of 1,296 aircraft are noted as airborne. (USAF)

▲31

▲32

▲33 ▼34

1,32,33. A Messerschmitt Bf 109 streams glycol and smoke as its ▶ilot bails out. During the last year of the war it was not unusual to ▶ncounter inexperienced German pilots who would not manoeuvre ▶ all as they were being attacked. (USAF)
4. A photo-reconnaissance Spitfire PR Mk.XI of the 7th Photo ▶roup somewhere over England. This high-altitude version of the ▶amous fighter could cruise above 40,000ft, which made it virtually ▶mmune from enemy interference over Germany. (Kay Bettin)
5. The 25th Bomb Group received Mk.XVI Mosquitoes in April

1944 for weather and reconnaissance flights over the Continent in support of 8th AF missions. This 654th Squadron aircraft has a number of missions under its belt and is still carrying invasion stripes under the wings and fuselage.
36. Replacement P-51Ds sit in the early morning fog along with a veteran P-51C. By the end of 1944 it was very unusual to see a 'razorback' Mustang in front-line service unless the aircraft happened to be a pilot's favourite. (Paul Coggan)

37. Liberators of the 467th Bomb Group drop their cargo, early 1945. The B-24 was able to carry a similar bomb load to the B-17 at rather better speed, but it was very heavy on the controls and a bad aircraft to belly-land since it broke apart. (Garry L. Fry)

38. A ground attack Fw 190F sits in the grass with its companions, awaiting another incursion by Allied troops and armour. Most of the initial batch of Focke Wulf attack pilots were originally trained on Ju 87 Stukas or Ju 88s; later, pilots of all types were placed in units regardless of training, often with disastrous results. (Alfred Price)

39. *14 Staffel* of *JG 3* at Gütersloh in December 1944: from left to right are Leipholz, Glaubig, Raab, Boesch, Schanz, Leuchtenberger and Gospers. These men were in the forefront opposing the Allied bombing effort in their Fw 190As during the period. (Oscar Boesch)

40. This Fw 190A-5/U9 packed quite a punch, with cannon and machine guns. Improvements visible include fairing doors for the wheels and a bulged, clear-vision canopy. (George Petersen)

◄37

38▼

39▼

40▼

▲41 ▼42

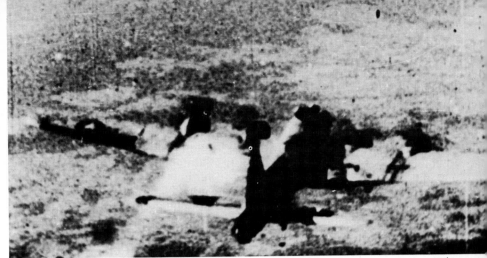

43▲

41. As ground attack became more important to the Luftwaffe in 1944 and 1945, the -F and -G versions of the Fw 190 took up much of the production line. The Fw 190G-8/R5 could carry bombs on five stations as well as multiple clusters on the centreline. (George Petersen)

42. The rocket-powered Messerschmitt Me 163B was introduced into combat in May 1944 and by the end of August it had surprised numerous 8th AF pilots. This *JG 400* Komet sits at Brandis, having just been fuelled; the chocks have been placed in front of the wheels, preparatory to a powered take-off.

43. Gun camera film from an Me 163 which has set the port wing of a B-17 on fire. The punch from the fighter's pair of 30mm cannon was effective if the pilot could hit his quarry at such high closing speeds.

44. Fw. Rudy Zimmerman's Me 163, photographed from Lt. Willard Erkamp's P-51 during a dogfight on 7 October 1944. The German crash-landed his damaged Komet and was able to run clear before strafing Mustangs wrecked the Messerschmitt on the ground. (USAF)

44▼

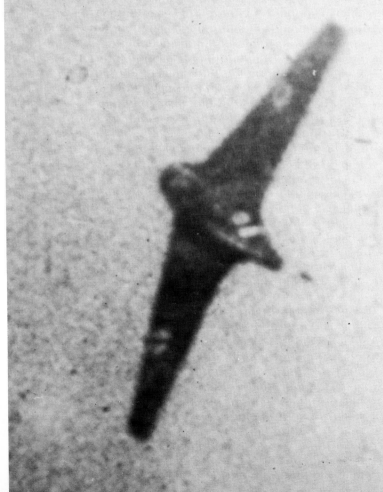

▲45

▲46　▼47

45. The 370th Squadron of the 359th Fighter Group encountered the Me 163 more than any other Allied combat unit. Three pilots who made 163 kills are in the picture: John Murphy, standing far right; Cyril Jones, leaning on the drop tank, third from left; and Ray Wetmore sitting on the wing, second from left. (John B. Murphy)

46. A 10th Photo Recon Group F-6D warms up for a tactical reconnaissance mission over enemy territory; with cameras in the rear fuselage and the normal six .50 calibre guns, this recce version of the Mustang had bite as well as vision The armament helped the aircraft to survive the low-level missions flown by 9th AF units. (USAF)

47. A 404th Fighter Group P-47D gets some attention at a forward base which used to be a Luftwaffe airfield. (Arthur O. Houston)

48. Lt. John H. Meyers looks back out of the 386th Bomb Group B-26 Marauder 'Hard Luck'. (Meyers via NASM)

49. A B-26G Marauder of the 386th BG in the late summer of 1944. The invasion stripes are well worn by this time. (Meyers via NASM)

▲50

▲51 ▼52

53 ▲

50. By 1945 the Thunderbolts of the 56th Fighter Group were camouflaged in a variety of schemes. The Wolfpack was the only 8th AF unit to retain P-47s until the end of the war. (George Bostwich via M. Olmsted)

51. A 404th FG Thunderbolt bombed up and ready for its next mission, 1945. (Moon via Sheflin/Olmsted)

52. Two flares are fired from a Flying Fortress as it comes in to land in England, indicating that there are wounded aboard. (USAF)

53. By late 1943 one of the premier photo-reconnaissance aircraft was the Lockheed F-5 Lightning, seen here finished in Synthetic Haze paint. (Lockheed-California Co.)

54. Though obsolete for much of the war, the Heinkel 111 continued to operate with many Luftwaffe units until the very end. (USAF)

54 ▼

▲55

▲56　▼57

55. The stop-gap Heinkel 162, though a delightful aircraft to fly, was not for the novice pilot as Hitler had intended. This aircraft flew operationally with *JG 1* during the final month of the war. (USAF)

56. The Arado Ar 234 jet bomber was the most successful of Hitler's advanced development aircraft at the end of the Second World War, and as a reconnaissance aircraft it was unequalled. (USAF)

57. B-17Gs of the 381st Bomb Group form up over England as an escorting P-47 hurries by. (USAF)

58. Almost every forward operating base occupied by the 9th Air Force was covered with pierced steel planking (PSP), seen here as this 36th Fighter Group Thunderbolt warms up. Though the temporary runway prevented aircraft from sinking into the mud, it did not prevent the mud from oozing up and turning the ground into a slick mess. (Arthur O. Houston)

59. The war almost over, Thunderbolts of the 397th Squadron, 404th Fighter Group, patrol out of Fritzlar, Germany, in April 1945. (Arthur O. Houston)

◀60
61▲ 62▼

60. Emil L. Sluga flew 'Slugger' with the 355th Fighter Group out of Steeple Morden. Note the two Spitfire rear-view mirrors, much sought after by American fighter pilots, along with RAF helmets, boots and gloves. (355th FG Assn.)

61. When Douglas A-26 Invaders began to replace B-26 Marauders in the 9th Air Force, pilots found an aircraft they loved as much as the one they gave up. Extremely fast, the A-26 could cruise at fighter speeds and carry a sizeable bomb load. These three Invaders sit at Straubing, Germany, along with a 368th Fighter Group AT-6. (Arthur O. Houston)

62. A 9th Air Force P-38 crash-lands after attacking targets during the advance of US infantry and armour in France. Anti-aircraft fire crippled the Lightning but it got home – note the bent propeller still sailing through the air amidst the dirt just behind the tail. (USAF)

▲63

63. P-51Ds of the 77th Squadron, 20th Fighter Group, in formation over England. One aircraft, LC-J, has had olive drab paint applied to the upper wing surfaces. Though many pilots were initially anxious about the bright aluminium finish of their aircraft in late 1944 and 1945, it seemed to make no difference to their kill ratios. (T. R. Bennett)

64. P-38s of the 474th Fighter Group taxi out on the grass for one of the final missions of the war, 20 April 1945. (USAF)

65. A 354th Fighter Group P-51D just about to touch down on the PSP at Ober Olm, Germany, 17 April 1945. Note the UC-78 'Bamboo Bomber' in the background. (USAF)

66. The 479th Fighter Group was the last to join the 8th Air Force, in May 1944, and made the last kill claimed by the 8th, on 25 April 1945. Instead of painting the noses of their Mustangs, Group pilots polished their spinners. (T. R. Bennett)

▼64

65 ▲

66 ▲

▲67

▲68 ▼69

34

7. Among the more distinctive 8th AF fighter units was the 55th Fighter Group, which often painted its green and yellow-nosed Mustangs with a swept olive drab theme that covered the rear fuselage and tail; they also painted their aircraft's namesake on the rudder. (T. R. Bennett)

8. Jim Gasser on 'short final' at Leiston in his 357th Fighter Group P-51D. The 357th was the first P-51 unit assigned to the 8th AF and claimed a higher rate of air victories than any other group during the final year of the war. (Merle Olmsted)

9. 'Jane' was the name given to all Bert Marshall's Mustangs while he flew with the 355th Fighter Group. After the war his aircraft was flown to a depot in Germany, and, like so many other wartime aircraft, it was scrapped. (Arthur D. Houston)

10. The 355th FG's 'Texas Terror IV' flies over England with field-applied olive drab on the upper fuselage, wings and tail. Note that the white in the national insignia has been toned down. (Bill Marshall)

11. On 18 August 1944 Bert Marshall (right) of the 355th Fighter Group was hit by anti-aircraft fire. After he belly-landed his P-51D in a large German hayfield, Royce Priest (left) landed his own Mustang near Marshall, put him in the single seat, then sat on his lap and took off after throwing both parachutes out to make room. (Bill Marshall)

70▲   71▼

▲72

72. P-51Ds of the 369th Squadron, 359th Fighter Group, climb out from their base at East Wretham, Norfolk. (Elmer Ward)

73. The 359th Fighter Group marked its fighters with downswept green noses in late 1944 and, along with other units in the 8th AF, removed the invasion stripes when Allied superiority was established over the Continent. (Elmer Ward)

74. Servicing the P-51 in combat was a task which often kept ground crews busy during the night. Here Hank Bille of the 357th

Squadron, 355th Fighter Group, adjusts his flight gear as the fuselage tank of his fighter is serviced at Steeple Morden in 1945. (Bill Marshall via Weidmann)

75. Mustangs of the 359th Fighter Group climb out above a broken cloud deck during a practice mission over England. (Elmer Ward)

76. On a rain-sodden taxiway at Leiston, 357th FG P-51Ds fitted with paper drop tanks prepare for an escort mission. (Arval Roberson)

▼73

74 ▲

75 ▲　76 ▼

77▲

77. The 15th Tac Recon Squadron line in 1945; note the cameras in the rear fuselage of the nearest aircraft. Attached to the 10th TRG, 9th Air Force, the unit operated under some very primitive conditions to fly its missions. (Carl Hildebrandt)

78. The 9th AF often coped with more mud than they thought possible, as this 354th FG Mustang shows. (Carl Hildebrandt)

79. As the razorback Mustangs became 'war weary' (denoted by 'WW' on their tails), several were converted to two-seaters. This 4th Fighter Group P-51B was very popular with ground crews at Debden since it provided a chance to fly in the aircraft they had worked on for so long. (Paul Betz)

WW312193

80. Flying Fortresses of the 100th Bomb Group high over Germany in 1945, long after the unit had earned its nickname of 'The Bloody Hundredth'. (Barney Lucas)
81. By 1945, weather no longer stopped the bombers since they could hit their targets through cloud by radar. This 303rd Bomb Group formation is over a solid cloud deck on 15 March 1945. (Barney Lucas)
82. Passing over contrails from preceding bombers, the 305th Bomb

Group approaches Plauen on 19 March 1945. Note the radar bombing scanner in place of the ball turret. (Barney Lucas)
83. With radar scanner extended, a 398th BG B-17 heads for Bremen, 30 March 1945. Though the Luftwaffe was still around during the last month of the war, the primary threat was the jet-powered Me 262, which was very effective during March and April. (Barney Lucas)

▲84 ▼85

42

86▲

86–87. One of the early production Me 262As, *WNr.* 170041, taxis out and takes off for a practice sortie while assigned to *Erprobungskommando 262*, the first Me 262 unit. Though the Jumo 004 engines lasted only 25 hours before needing overhaul, the jet fighter's speed and four 30mm cannon made it extremely effective when flown by an experienced pilot, although it was not until the end of the war that its potential was beginning to be exploited. (Via Ken Bokleman)

87▼

▲88

88. Though the wings of the Me 262 were only mildly swept, this led to excellent high-speed performance and good control harmony, and leading-edge slats, which deployed at low speeds, provided good control for landing. The only major problem in flying the aircraft centred around the handling of the throttles: the engines could be flamed out or overheated if not used with caution. (National Archives)

89,90. The most successful German jet design of the war was the Arado 234 reconnaissance bomber aircraft. Here the prototype Ar 234, which released a dolly on take-off and landed on a skid, flies a test mission. The world's first jet reconnaissance mission was flown by Lt. Erich Sommer over Normandy on 2 August 1944 with complete impunity since no Allied fighters could climb and catch him. (National Archives)

91. Preparing a B-17 for combat took many hours of work on the ground. Mechanical problems, mud and bad weather all hindered operations. (USAF)

▲89   ▼90

91▶

44

◀92   93▲

94▲

92. This view of 381st BG Fortresses over England shows what kind of wear and tear aircraft took if they lasted through combat. Not only is the paint on VP-X well worn and faded, but outer wing panels from an entirely different aircraft have been fitted. (USAF)

93. A 653rd Squadron, 25th Bomb Group, Mosquito PR.XVI painted overall in PRU Blue. This unit flew weather and reconnaissance missions for the 8th Air Force through to the end of the war. (Garry L. Fry)

94. Liberators of the 93rd Bomb Group head for their target, 1945. The lead aircraft has bombing radar, which enabled the 8th Air Force to deliver their loads regardless of the weather below. (USAF)

95. The P-61 Black Widow became a very effective night fighter during the last year of the war. It was the first aircraft to be designed specifically for the night fighting mission, and it was the first US aircraft to use spoilers for ailerons. (USAF)

95▼

96. A 4th FG Mustang is fitted with 108-gallon paper drop tanks at Debden. These long-range tanks were the ideal solution to the problem of conserving strategic materials since not only were they easy to make (out of compressed paper), but they also were inexpensive. (USAF)

97. An early Fw 190D-9 assigned to *JG 3*. The 'long-nose' Focke Wulf was equal to anything the Allies were flying and it was a tricky opponent. (Alfred Price)

98. Beginning with the 12th Air Force, the USAAF started to hit German targets from the Mediterranean Theatre of Operations (MTO) in order to pound the enemy on two sides, with the Russians hitting from a third side. Here, a 320th Bomb Group Marauder is en route over Florence, Italy, to hit German installations. (USAF)

▲99

▲100

99. One of about a dozen Halifax bombers which flew missions out of the American base at Foggia, Italy, in 1944. In the background are 325th Fighter Group P-47s. (Charles H. Brown)

100. A great success with the 12th and 15th Air Forces in the Mediterranean, the P-38 provided long-range escort for the Fortresses and Liberators. These 27th Squadron, 1st Fighter Group, P-38Js are heading back home, less their drop tanks. (Francis J. Pope)

101. Tightly formed up under the waist of a B-17, these 94th Squadron, 1st FG, Lightnings provide some comfort on the last stretch home. (USAF)

102. 'Big friend' – 'little friend': a 1st Fighter Group Lightning shepherds a 99th Bomb Group Fortress back to base after a 15th Air Force 'maximum effort'. (USAF)

101▲   102▼

▲103 ▼104

105 ▲

103. What a sight! Lightnings cross over protectively as the 2nd Bomb Group heads for Linz, Austria, on 8 January 1945. Though the twin contrails showed bomber crews that the approaching fighter was friendly, they also pointed out the Lightnings to German fighter pilots. (USAF)

104. Escort in reverse. These 20th Squadron, 2nd BG, B-17Gs are escorting a 1st Fighter Group P-38J back home after it was hit by flak over Bleckhammer, Germany, on 7 July 1944. The pilot feathered the right engine after losing oil, then tucked in with the Forts for the long trip home. (USAF)

105. Francis J. Pope, commander of the 27th Squadron, 1st Fighter Group, flies his P-38J over Foggia, Italy, in 1944. (Francis J. Pope)

106. A 500lb bomb is winched on to a 94th Fighter Squadron Lightning at Foggia in the early morning. The P-38's load-carrying capability made it an excellent fighter-bomber and dive-bomber, so it was often used to hit both tactical and strategic targets. (USAF)

106 ▼

▲107

107. The 325th Fighter Group became known as the 'Checkertails', for obvious reasons. They found that their long-range Mustangs would take them from Italy into the deepest parts of the Reich. (T. R. Bennett)

108. Art Fiedler's 325th FG Mustang being run up for an escort mission out of Italy to Germany. The large drop tanks enabled the fighters to stay with the bombers all the way to the target and back, much to the chagrin of the Luftwaffe (Art Fiedler via Hess)

109. 'Nita VII' was the personal aircraft of the 15th Air Forces' 306th Fighter Wing commander Col. Yantis H. Taylor. The tail markings of all four fighter groups under his control are painted in a diamond on the tail. (Art Fiedler via Hess)

110. Pierced Steel Planking was used everywhere in Italy, a haven for mud. This Mustang pilot has just initiated undercarriage retraction – the clamshell inboard doors are snapping open to receive the main gear. (USAF)

▼108

▲111 ▼112

56

111. Lt. Bernard L. Ball's 449th Bomb Group Liberator received a flak burst in the waist section during a 15th AF 'bridge busting' mission. The rudder cables were severed and one crew member was killed, but, using differential engine power, Ball brought the bomber home. (USAF)
112. Two 451st BG B-24s head north for Germany over the quilted Italian landscape. (USAF)

113. Having careered off the runway after landing with the port main gear still up, a B-24 of the 450th BG grinds to a stop in the dust at a base in Italy. Flak has riddled the ship's vital systems. (USAF)
114. A 301st Bomb Group B-17 ploughs through mud and water – in spite of the PSP – and heads for Austria. (USAF)

▲115

115. A 97th BG Flying Fortress is met by an ambulance at Amendola, Italy. The group has just returned from hitting the ball-bearing works at Steyr, Austria. (USAF)

116. Maj. Bradford Evans, on his 46th mission, tries to get his burning 99th B-17 down after crossing the Alps back to Italy from Toulon, France. (USAF)

▼116

117. As this 97th BG B-17G was landing it caught fire, but Air Service Command firefighters tackled it quickly and, despite heavy damage to the right wing, the bomber was put back into service. (USAF)
118. Florence, Italy, November 1944: crew chief Ralph Willett (right) stands in front of his 12th Squadron, 3rd Photo Group, F-5E Lightning. This 12th Air Force group flew continually over German-held territory. (Ralph Willett)

118▼

119. B-25Js of the 12th Air Force's 319th Bomb Group on the way to their base at Corsica in December 1944. The Mitchell medium bomber proved to be a rugged aircraft which was easy to fly and maintain. (USAF)

▲120

120. 'Leaflet bombing' was a mission flown by every air force: these 12th AF 340th BG Mitchells are on their way back from Germany after a leaflet run. The crews are obviously making a statement about their feelings in dropping such harmless cargo – each starboard engine is shut down and the propellers are feathered! (USAF)

121. A 487th Squadron, 340th Bomb Group, B-25J heads out over the mountains of northern Italy to hit the German bridge at San Michelle, on the Brenner Line, 22 January 1945. The Brenner Pass

was one of three vital supply routes to the Germans in Italy. (USAF)

122. A 12th AF B-25, hit by an 88mm flak burst over Yugoslavia. For more than two hours the pilot and co-pilot wrestled with the bomber to bring it to friendly territory. (USAF)

123. Mitchells of the 12th AF on their way to rail targets over northern Italy. The B-25 was so stable that it could almost be 'parked' in formation during long flights, though no pilot would ever say it was easy! (USAF)

▼121

122▲   123▼

63

124. 319th BG B-25Js head out over the sea in the early morning, northern Italy, 1945. (USAF)

125. Mitchells of the 340th Bomb Group over the Italian Alps en route to the Brenner Pass, 1945. The 'soft underbelly' of Italy was anything but that, as the Germans continued to resist until the very end. (USAF)

125▲

126. Three-ship box elements were standard in almost all AAF bomb groups whatever the theatre since the formation provided mutual protection, using all the guns in the flight. These 319th BG Mitchells are in excellent position as the low box of the formation. (USAF)

126▼

▲127

127. With only the nosewheel partially down, this crippled 310th Bomb Group B-25J, nicknamed 'Angel of Mercy', is about to crash-land in Italy after a rough mission. Enemy flak destroyed the hydraulic system, and the crew could only get partial flaps and the nosewheel loose; the main gear never budged. After sliding to a stop, the aircraft's only noticeable damage was bent engine mounts. (USAF)

128. A 414th Night Fighter Squadron P-61 Black Widow cruises north out of Italy in the late evening at the start of a mission. This big fighter was manoeuvrable and very lethal, with four 20mm cannon and four .50 calibre machine guns. (USAF)

129. A 340th Bomb Group, 486th Squadron, B-25J in trouble: 'Yankee Doodle Dandy' has just taken a direct hit in the port engine over the target, 13 February 1945. The Mitchell went down almost immediately. (John Sutay Jr.)

130. An Fw 190 is run up by AAF pilots in Germany. As the war ended, literally thousands of Luftwaffe aircraft littered the countryside and many were flown, both for test purposes and for fun. (A. Hess Bomberger)

▼128

132. A 414th Squadron Black Widow warms up in the Italian night prior to taking off on a long-range prowl for German aircraft. (USAF)

131. The morning after: two 9th Air Force P-61s in France after returning from a night sortie on 27 September 1944. From July 1944 to May 1945 the 422nd and 425th Night Fighter Squadrons claimed a total of 57 enemy aircraft in the air. (USAF)

▲133

▲134 ▼135

133. Germany's attempt to equal the Mosquito in the night sky was the Ta 154 Moskito. It failed, though it was a beautiful aircraft. Here the V7 prototype rests at Langenhagen, the Focke-Wulf test field. (George Petersen)

134. An Me 109 of the Croatian Air Force, surrendered at Falconara, Italy, 16 April 1945. (USAF)

135. Me 262B night fighters from *NJG 11* flew in defence of Berlin achieving a number of kills. Here, one is inspected postwar, 6 June 1945. (USAF)

136. Fritzlar, Germany after the surrender in May 1945. The field is filled with Me 110 night fighters, being inspected here by 368th Group pilot Mark Cauble. (Arthur O. Houston)

137. 368th FG P-47 pilot Arthur Houston looks over one of the Me 109s left behind at Fritzlar. The aircraft were in excellent shape. (Arthur O. Houston)

136▲ 137▼

▲138
138. This He 162A, 'yellow 4' of *3/JG 1*, was one of many prizes found by the Allies when hostilities were over. *JG 2* saw limited combat with its hastily constructed Heinkel jets – a last gasp for a
▼139

dying empire. (NASM)
139. The end of Hitler's Reich, upon which the cream of the Luftwaffe was sacrificed. (A. Hess Bomberger)